Pam

Pam

Pam sips.

Pam nips.

Pam sits.

Sam and Dan pat Pam.

12

Nat pats Sam
and Dan.

Pat, pat, pat.

Before reading

Say the sounds: s a t p i n m d

Practise blending the sounds: sips pat pats Pat sits sit Dan Pam Sam Nat nips

High-frequency words: and

Vocabulary check: nip – a small bite

Story discussion: Look at the cover. Who is this story about? What can you tell about this dog?

Teaching points: Remind children about the use of capital letters for names. Talk about the verb "pat" and how with the addition of "s", it becomes pats. Introduce speech bubbles as a way to show what a character is saying.

After reading

Comprehension:
- Who are the characters in this book?
- What is the name of the dog?
- What are some of the things Pam can do?
- Who does Nat pat?

Fluency: Speed read the words again from the inside front cover.